THE CELTIC YEAR

FOLKLORE, MYTHS AND MAGIC

THE CELTIC YEAR

FOLKLORE, MYTHS AND MAGIC

ALISON DAVIES

Illustrated by
Megan Ivy Griffiths

Quadrille

WELCOME

Step back through the annals of time, beyond the swirling mists that gathered over mountain and moor, to when great plateaus of land covered the earth, and ancient forests spread like moss over hill and valley. Picture the landscape wild and free, an untamed tangle of vegetation with vast sprawling meadows and fields, and you will have some idea of what it was like for the Celtic people, and of how they felt growing up in this space. Described as 'barbarians' by the ancient Greeks who first encountered them on the southern coast of France around 540 BCE, they called them Keltoi, a name that evolved into the more familiar term, Celts.

Nomadic in spirit, this was a people who were meant to roam and cover a wide expanse, from Spain to the Black Sea. They were the largest group to inhabit Western and Central Europe, later venturing to the British Isles where they set up home during the Iron Age, through the Roman Age and beyond. While their fierce reputation helped them dominate and retain territory, this collection of tribes, who often fought between themselves, had a deeply spiritual connection to the world around them. They understood that in order to survive and thrive, they would need to work with nature, synching with the cycles of the seasons and taking their lead from the creatures of the earth.

They lived in settlements, clusters of roundhouses usually located within large hillforts, where they could nurture the land, keep their cattle and cultivate crops. While they weren't averse to battle, for the most part they were farmers and labourers. Within each group there were the seers, the rule-makers and the spell-casters. Known as Druids, these learned souls studied the natural world, taking inspiration from the planets and stars, and charting their path through the sky. They calculated the length of the seasons, the meaning of each subtle change, and harnessed the healing medicine of plants and trees. They invented rites that embraced the power of nature, and most importantly they told their stories, spreading words of wisdom amid oral history to create some of the most famous myths and legends in the world today. It's no wonder then that we are enchanted by this mysterious group, who never had an empire as such, but learned to co-exist within the territories they had established.

Within the pages of this book, you'll discover the secrets of the Celts laid out in a month-by-month structure, which embodies the way they worked with the shifting seasons. You will be introduced to the myths, traditions, practices and folklore at the heart of their beliefs; the things that motivated them; the four major fire festivals they prized above anything else; and the sense of unity that each tribe worked to create to establish harmony and a unified goal.

You will learn about the Celtic tree signs, which follow a thirteen-month lunar year, and how each of the trees held meaning and power for the Druids. You will uncover some of the most popular gods and goddesses, and the stories associated with them. You'll also learn how to work with these deities through simple rituals that connect you with their energy. The symbols that were significant to the Celts are also highlighted, and you will learn how to harness their power for yourself. From sacred sites to monthly spells, you'll gain a greater understanding of how the Celts navigated daily life, and how the natural world was key to their success.

This book takes you on a journey so that you can develop your own way of connecting with nature inspired by the ancients, and draw upon their customs and traditions.

Turn the page, turn back time, and welcome to *The Celtic Year*.

THE WHEEL OF THE YEAR

This seasonal calendar, which was arranged in a circular formation to portray the continuous turn of a wheel and the cyclical nature of existence, was embraced by the Celts, and provided a blueprint from which they could live by. They used it to mark the passing of time and divided it into sections to represent the seasons and honour key solar events.

Split into two halves to signify the light and dark halves of the year, the wheel also featured the winter and summer solstice, known as Yule and Litha, and the spring and autumn equinox, also called Ostara and Mabon. These festivals, often referred to as quarter festivals, symbolize the transition of time and the shifting of seasons, and make up four of the eight celebrations highlighted.

The remaining four, which are Imbolc, Beltane, Lughnasadh and Samhain, are key fire festivals. Each had its own specific themes and attributes, but the one thing they all had in common was the opportunity to take a step back and give thanks for the gifts of the season. For a race that lived so intrinsically with nature, it was important to observe these cyclical transitions, and celebrate each turn of the wheel.

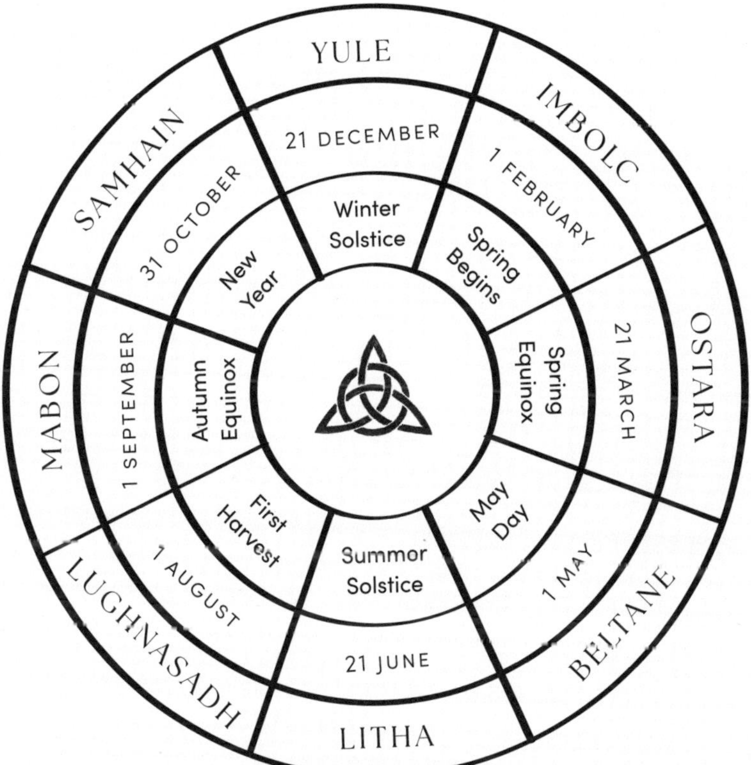
YULE
21 DECEMBER
Winter Solstice
IMBOLC
1 FEBRUARY
Spring Begins
OSTARA
21 MARCH
Spring Equinox
BELTANE
1 MAY
May Day
LITHA
21 JUNE
Summer Solstice
LUGHNASADH
1 AUGUST
First Harvest
MABON
1 SEPTEMBER
Autumn Equinox
SAMHAIN
31 OCTOBER
New Year

WIN

TER

As autumn rolls over, it lands with grace upon winter's snow-lined path. The chill has set in and the darkness, which once lingered in the shadows, finally finds its strength, moving with stealth through the barren landscape. The skeletal trees become silent sentinels, marking time and place. There is space to breathe here and to withdraw and contemplate the inner and outer world.

The tribe hunkers down, taking inspiration from furry and feathered friends. The tribe nestles within walls lined with mud, straw and wattle, and animal hides and blankets draped over tunics provide protection from the season's hungry bite. Bards extol the virtues of the longest night and the shortest day, while the Druids make sacred oaths to recognize the power of rebirth at the heart of winter's grip. At every turn of the wheel, there is something to celebrate, and a gift to be gleaned and revered for its beauty.

DECEMBER

CELTIC FOLKLORE

ALBAN ARTHAN

The winter solstice was a time of celebration, and a key moment in the Druids' calendar. Marking the shortest day and the longest night, this event was called Alban Arthan, meaning 'light of winter' in Welsh, although it has many other Celtic names. According to ancient beliefs, it was at this point in the year when the endless battle between the Oak King and the Holly King reached its climax.

The Holly King was synonymous with the old year and the shortened days, thanks to the diminishing light of the sun, while the Oak King represented the new year to come and the return of the sun. According to legend, the Holly King, who assumed power around the autumn equinox, remained evergreen through the harsh mid-winter months, but was finally defeated as the shortest day moved into the longest night. From this point the Oak King reigned supreme, bringing with him the hope of renewed light and warmth, and the return of the spring. The Celts associated the wren with the Holly King and the robin with the Oak King, a reference to when the birds were most active in the year.

It was thought that the sun stood still during the twelve days of Yule, the winter festival which begins at the eve of the winter solstice, and for those days the tribes would gather and create a communal fire. Each family would add logs to the pyre to encourage the sun to move and grow in strength.

TREE OF THE MONTH

ELDER

Birth Sign Dates: 25 November - 23 December

The elder tree marked the darkest phase of the year, and was associated with death, rebirth and wisdom. The Druids were particularly fond of its healing powers, using all parts, from the bark to the leaves and fruit, to make tinctures and teas to reduce fever, soothe bruises and alleviate infection. The berries were considered the most magical part of the tree, and any fruit left hanging from its boughs in December was highly prized and thought to be a gift from the mother goddess. Elder leaves were often carved into funerary flints and stones to mark the soul's safe passage on to the next life.

Freedom-loving and adventurous, those born under this tree sign like to push boundaries and take risks. Life is for living, and elder personalities make the most of every second. While they can be exhibitionists, they do have a quieter side and often withdraw from their nearest and dearest to reflect and recharge. Their impulsive nature and quirky personality make life fun for those who know them.

CELTIC DEITY

CERIDWEN

The Celtic goddess of the Underworld, Ceridwen, was associated with death, rebirth, transformation and magic. A gifted sorceress, she was the keeper of the Cauldron of Inspiration and Knowledge, and renowned for her ability to shapeshift into any form. Often depicted as an old and wizened hag, in truth, Ceridwen was incredibly beautiful. She had two children: a girl named Creidwy, a radiant being that shone with light and love, and a boy called Afagddu who was the opposite, evil and full of darkness. To cure her son of his maleficence she created a potion in her cauldron, a powerful spell that needed a year and a day to bubble away. She asked her servant Gwion Bach to stir the pot for her every day. On the very last day when the potion came to potency, three drops splashed onto Gwion's thumb. He immediately put it in his mouth to soothe the burn and swallowed the potion.

Gwion knew that Ceridwen would be enraged by this, so he tried to escape using his newly acquired powers to shift into the form of a rabbit. Ceridwen transformed into a greyhound to pursue him. Gwion quickly leapt into the river and shifted into a fish, but Ceridwen was ready and turned into an otter. He changed into bird, and she became a hawk. Finally, in desperation, he turned into a grain of corn, but clever Ceridwen transformed into a hen and ate him. She later gave birth to another son who was a reincarnation of Gwion: a beautiful baby filled with light and inspiration who became Taliesin the bard.

DEITY RITUAL

RITUAL FOR PSYCHIC POWERS

Ceridwen was adept at divination, and would use her cauldron to see visions of the future, adding herbs and other magical ingredients to the mix to enhance her psychic powers. This practice is known as scrying.

Take inspiration from this goddess and create your own cauldron of truth to help focus your mind and glean insights for the future.

You will need: a dark bowl (preferably black or dark blue), a piece of amethyst, a lighter or matches, a candle

- ∞ To begin, cleanse the bowl by leaving it outside on a rainy day. The fresh water will purify it, ready for use. A dark-coloured bowl is ideal, as it doesn't reflect the light and makes the perfect canvas for you to see shapes and patterns at a later stage in the ritual.
- ∞ Retrieve the bowl and place a piece of amethyst in it. Amethyst is renowned for its ability enhance intuition.
- ∞ Fill the bowl with water, making sure the stone is covered.
- ∞ Light a candle and set the intention that you would like to receive insights, wisdom and psychic messages.
- ∞ Sit with the bowl in front of you. Take your time and focus on the surface of the water. You're going to try to see images in the water's surface. It's likely that you won't see much at first, but try to relax and soften your gaze.
- ∞ Let thoughts come and go, but take note of them. Your intuition will speak to you in images, thoughts and feelings.
- ∞ Spend five to ten minutes scrying, and then record anything that seems significant.

SACRED SITE

FANUM D'ARON

Aurillac, France

The Fanum d'Aron ruins at Aurillac, situated in the Auvergne region of France, were an important part of Celtic worship. The word *fanum* means 'sacred space', and this was once a grand and carefully planned Romano-Celtic temple, which over time fell to ruins and lay almost forgotten. Rediscovered in 1970, the main body of the temple was then excavated. Remnants such as rock sculptures and ceramics suggest the temple was in use from the 1st to 3rd centuries.

SYMBOL

CELTIC CROSS

Depicted as a cross with a circle over the centre intersection, the Celtic cross has been in existence for thousands of years. Early interpretations, called sun crosses, have been found throughout Europe dating back to the 5th century. Synonymous with strength, knowledge and compassion, it's believed that this symbol evolved from a traditional Christian cross, and that the nimbus in the centre, which was added during the early Middle Ages, represents the sun's power and eternal light. As Christianity spread, the cross took on new meaning, becoming a symbol of faith and a link between divinity and humankind.

SYMBOL RITUAL

RITUAL FOR STRENGTH AND PURPOSE

One of the simplest symbols to recall and draw, the Celtic cross celebrates our connection to the Universe. It can be used as a blueprint to draw strength and energy, and align you with your true purpose.

- ∞ Stand with your feet together and your shoulders back. Lift your chin slightly and tuck your tummy in. Imagine being stretched into a long thin line, and elongate your spine.
- ∞ Take a deep breath in and raise your arms out to the sides in a straight line to create a cross shape.
- ∞ As you exhale, imagine a huge disc of golden light resting on top of your head. Feel it descending until it covers the upper part of your body and you are encased in a halo of light.
- ∞ Inhale and feel the radiant glow of the light infuse you with hope and vitality.
- ∞ Exhale and feel your connection to the Universe, and your surroundings strengthen.
- ∞ Continue to breathe in this way, holding the position you have created for at least a minute.
- ∞ When you're ready, bring your arms down to your sides. Relax, and give your body a gentle shake to finish.

MONTHLY SPELL

SPELL TO PROMOTE HARMONY AND GOOD FORTUNE

The Celts embraced the flow of the seasons. They knew which plants grew at each point in the year, and they worked with nature's offerings to create magical rituals and spells.

Use the plants of the season in a spell to promote happiness and attract good fortune into your home.

You will need: a length of gold ribbon, frankincense essential oil, gardening gloves, a sprig of mistletoe, a sprig of holly

∞ Take the gold ribbon and sprinkle a couple of drops of the frankincense oil onto it. Frankincense has an uplifting scent that attracts luck and positive energy.

∞ Take the sprigs of mistletoe and holly, both associated with happiness and protection, and tie them together using the scented ribbon. You may like to wear gardening gloves while doing this to protect yourself from the holly spikes. As you tie the plants together, think about the type of good fortune that you'd like to attract and what this would look like for you. For example, if you want to attract abundance and create a happy home, you might see everyone getting on and your home filled with lots of lovely things.

∞ Once you have finished tying the sprigs together, say, 'A sprig of luck, a sprig of love, and countless blessings from above'.

∞ Hang the magical decoration above your front door.

JANUARY

CELTIC MYTH

THE ANKOU

In the dark of winter at the dead of night, if you happen to be outside, then you might encounter the Ankou. According to the Celtic people of Brittany known as the Bretons, this skeletal figure, sheathed in a long coat and a wide-brimmed hat, would wield his scythe while gathering the souls of the dead. He travelled upon a rickety old cart drawn by four black horses, which clattered through the streets to herald his arrival. Supposedly, the Ankou is the latest person to die in a village, who then assumes the role of deathly summoner.

According to one Breton legend, three drunken friends were coming home one night when they encountered a frail old man sitting upon his broken cart. Two of the men began throwing stones and yelling, while the third took pity on him and tried to mend his coach. The next day, the two who had thrown stones were found dead in their beds. The third, who had tried to help the Ankou, escaped this fate, although his hair had turned white as snow overnight.

TREES OF THE MONTH

BIRCH

Birth Sign Dates: 24 December - 20 January

Often called the Lady of the Woods by the Celts, the birch tree symbolizes rebirth and an awakening, as the earth gently stirs beneath winter's icy cover. Birch rods were used in love rites and rituals, and young couples would leap over them to cement their union. The twigs of this tree were also crafted into bridal dolls. To the Druids, this tree was synonymous with protection and purification.

Those born under this tree sign are high achievers and natural born leaders. Birch characters are able to take control in a crisis and remain unflappable, and they are gifted with charm and the ability to lift others. Those who embody the qualities of this tree are strong and resilient, and always looking to create a better future.

ROWAN

Birth Sign Dates: 21 January - 17 February

Known as the Tree of Life to the Celts, the rowan is imbued with mystical energy. With its creamy white flowers in spring and bright red berries in autumn, this tree is distinctive and prefers to grow at higher altitudes. A favourite of the Druids, rowan twigs and sticks were burned in protective rituals and carried as a way of warding off evil. The wood of the rowan was thought to promote psychic energy when kept close. Commonly planted near dwellings, this tree was a hardy sentinel watching over the spirits of the dead, and would often appear at burial sites and cemeteries.

Cool and calm, those born under this tree sign can appear aloof at first glance. But don't be fooled. They are extremely passionate and often have deep yearnings and desires. This sign has a keen, perceptive mind and is able to judge a situation and sense subtle changes in the atmosphere.

CELTIC DEITY

DANU

The earth goddess Danu was of great importance to the Celts. Her influence could be felt across Eastern Europe through to the emerald isle of Ireland, where she was thought to be the mother of a legendary tribe of fairy folk known as the Tuatha Dé Danann, meaning 'People of the Goddess Danu'. In this role she was gifted with magic and infinite wisdom, which she put to good use, suckling both the earth and the gods to create a lush and abundant landscape.

Known as a principal deity, she was also associated with the wind and free-flowing bodies of water. Indeed, many scholars believe that the goddess was a spiritual manifestation of one of the longest rivers in Europe. Thought to be a sovereign with noble blood, Danu was called upon by many rulers for gifts and blessings. Standing stones and wells were common sites of worship for this goddess.

DEITY RITUAL

RITUAL FOR SELF-CARE AND ENERGY

Connect with the magical energy of Danu with a ritual that focuses on self-care, and nurturing body and mind.

Danu shifts between the elements of earth, air and water, letting her energy flow to replenish each one. You can do the same by getting out into nature and engaging your senses.

∞ Wrap up warm on a brisk windy day and go for a walk in your local park or nature reserve. Choose somewhere that has access to a lake, stream or pond so that you can be close to water.

∞ Take your time and enjoy the experience. Think about each of the elements as you stroll.

∞ Notice what you can see, how the wind buffets the trees and branches, how the earth responds to the breeze and how the water swirls beneath gusts of air.

∞ Engage your other senses. Think about what you can hear, the sound of wind as it rustles the leaves, the noise your feet make as they connect with the earth, and the gentle trickle of a stream.

∞ Consider what you can smell and taste, the fresh scent of the air, the mossy ground and perhaps the dampness of a recent downpour.

∞ Breathe deeply, drawing the air in through your nose and out of your mouth. Let each breath still your thoughts.

∞ Allow the stresses of the day to slip away as you drink in the environment.

SACRED SITE

THE CARNAC STANDING STONES

Brittany, France

The megaliths of Carnac are a prominent feature from ancient Brittany. Known as the Carnac Alignments, they are split into several sections, which are now divided by trees and roads. Following a coastal path, the stones meander and extend over four miles, covering an impressive swathe of land, which might once have marked a border between land and sea. Theories abound as to their meaning, with some citing the menhirs, which are large upright standing stones, as a ceremonial tool for sun and moon worship. In other tales, they are goblin-like creatures made of stone, while some stories suggest that the menhirs were once a Roman army transformed by Druidic magic.

SYMBOL

THE AWEN

Often called the three rays of light, the awen is a popular symbol, which was created by the 18th-century Welsh poet and Druid, Iolo Morganwg. The word awen itself is much older. Featuring in the Celtic language, it means 'inspiration', and was used to define the spark of an idea or the creative flow experienced by poets and bards. Traditionally, the image was comprised of three rays of light, which appear to spring forth from three small dots, each of which represent truth, balance and existence.

To the Druids, it's synonymous with the life essence of nature and the breath of the divine. Although there are varying interpretations of the rays, each one depicts a different aspect such as mind, body and spirit, or land, sea and sky.

SYMBOL RITUAL

RITUAL FOR CREATIVITY

Harness the energy of this symbol when you want to tap into your creative side by using the symbol to trigger your imagination.

You will need: an image of the awen symbol, a few pieces of paper and a pen

∞ Spend some time in quiet reflection gazing at the image of the symbol.

∞ Consider what the three rays of light might mean to you and write down three words that instantly come to mind when you think of the symbol. It doesn't matter what you write, just let your imagination take over.

∞ Look at the words and think of another three words. Write these down.

∞ Read all the words you have written so far, and think of another three words associated with your musings. Soon you will have a page of words, all born from the same symbol.

∞ Read through them and you may notice a pattern developing.

∞ Now, challenge yourself to write a short poem or paragraph using some of the words that you have noted down. Have fun with this. It doesn't matter what you write, the point is that you are exercising your imagination and allowing your creativity to flow.

MONTHLY SPELL

SPELL FOR INNER STRENGTH AND PROTECTION

The Celts were inspired by objects that they found in nature, and often used them in sacred rituals and as charms. This spell also uses a gift of the natural world to help you feel safe and strong.

You will need: a small to medium stone from your garden, or found on a walk

- To begin, you will need to infuse your stone with moonlight. Take the stone outside at night and hold it in both hands. Close your eyes and say, 'Hard as stone, strong and true, I draw your strength in all I do'. Leave the stone somewhere overnight that you can easily find again.
- In the morning when the sun has risen, retrieve the stone.
- Stand beneath the light of the sun's rays and say, 'Hard as stone, strong and true, I draw your strength in all I do'. Leave the stone in the sunlight for the rest of the day.
- In the evening after sunset, retrieve the stone for a final time and keep it with you as a charm for strength and protection.
- Whenever you feel vulnerable, hold the stone in both hands and repeat the magical affirmation, 'Hard as stone, strong and true, I draw your strength in all I do'.

FEBRUARY

CELTIC FESTIVAL

IMBOLC

On the 1st February each year the Celts would celebrate Imbolc, a festival that marked the return of the sun's radiant light and the potential of spring. The name itself means 'in the belly' or 'in the womb', and refers to new life stirring beneath the surface of the earth and the milk-laden udders of expectant ewes at that time.

Imbolc draws a line between the winter solstice and the vernal equinox of the spring, and signals new beginnings. To the Celts it was a time of feasting, preparing the land ready for new growth and sowing seeds for the future. Not only was the land warming up after winter's harsh chill, but the animals that had gone into hibernation were slowly emerging from their slumber, and much of the livestock were pregnant.

Imbolc was a fire festival, and one of the main traditions at that time was to light fires and dance around them. The Celts associated this festival with their much-loved goddess Brigid. She was the deity of the hearth and fire, synonymous with healing, fertility, poetry and smithcraft. As the influence of Christianity grew, the festival became known as St Brigid's Day.

TREE OF THE MONTH

ASH

Birth Sign Dates: 18 February - 17 March

Known as *uinseann* in Irish, the ash tree was sacred to the Celts. They revered its legendary size, believing it was a bridge between realms. The height, which could reach over 180 feet (55 metres), wasn't the only thing that caught their eye. Being so lofty, the ash was a prime target for lightning bolts, which meant it was connected to the elements of air and fire while also being of the earth. The wood was highly esteemed for this reason, and many tribes used it to craft spears and staffs, believing them to be imbued with the magic of the tree.

The enchanting souls born under this tree sign have a rich imagination, and can be artistic. They love to engage with the world around them and find solace in nature. While ash personalities have their head in the clouds for much of the time, they are also inspiring to be around, as they see the beauty in everything.

CELTIC DEITY

THE CAILLEACH

The mysterious Cailleach, also known as the Hag and the Veiled One, was the queen of the winter months. A goddess who controlled the cold harsh weather, the biting winds and the snow, she could even influence the length of the season and the darkness of the days. Appearing as an elderly woman swathed in a shadowy cloak, she had one eye, which gleamed through the darkness, and skin as pale as the moon. It was thought that she could ride storms and control the elements.

While many tales depict her as a fearsome creature, in truth she was neither good nor evil. She lived in the wild places and protected the land, sometimes shielding the earth from destruction, sometimes causing it. A patron of wolves, it's thought she loved wild animals. In Scottish folklore she was a deer herder. Some legends attest that when the spring returned, the Cailleach was restored to her youthful form. During Imbolc, this goddess was most active, gathering firewood for the rest of the year.

DEITY RITUAL

RITUAL FOR POSITIVITY

The Cailleach had a well, which she drew water from every day. She covered the opening with a slab of stone, and some days she would leave the slab to one side and let the water spill over and flood the land.

Harness the power of this goddess with this simple water ritual to embrace the cycles of life, and imbue you with positive energy.

You will need: lavender essential oil, a cup

∞ Half fill your sink with warm water, then add three to four drops of lavender essential oil to the water. Lavender is soothing and has uplifting properties.

∞ Swirl the water with your hands in a clockwise circular motion. As you do this, think about the cycles in your life and how they ebb and flow.

∞ Think about the movement of the seasons and how winter flows into spring, spring into summer and so on. Nothing stays the same; the world is made up of fluid movement taking you from one cycle to the next.

∞ Take a cup and fill it from the sink, then gently pour the water over your arms and hands. Imagine that like the Cailleach, you are drawing healing water from the well to cleanse yourself.

∞ Say, 'Positive energy flows through me, as I move with the ebb and flow of life'.

SACRED SITE

ST BRIGID'S WELL

Clare, Ireland

One of the most mystical spots on the west coast of Ireland, St Brigid's Well, is entombed in an ancient stone grotto. The gentle trickle of the sacred waters can still be heard in this holy place, and it's easy to imagine the rituals that were held for the goddess here. While Brigid has many wells dedicated to her name, this one is by far the most intriguing. Above it lies a cemetery, the resting place of many clan leaders and mythical kings, and the tree-lined path that leads there is adorned with votives in the form of clothing and rosaries. The grotto itself is home to thousands of prayers and mementos, left in exchange for a blessing from the goddess.

SYMBOL

ST BRIGID'S CROSS

Usually made from interwoven rushes, this national symbol of Ireland has ancient Celtic roots. The cross itself, which has four arms protruding from a central, patterned square, was displayed on doors to protect a home and its occupants from fire, evil and hunger. A potent symbol of forthcoming spring, it was crafted with love and care during Imbolc and then hung on or near the entrance to a dwelling.

Brigid was a Celtic fire goddess of healing who was adopted by the Christian faith and turned into a saint to ease the transition from Celtic beliefs and customs into the new religion. According to Celtic legend, Brigid was called upon to sit by the bed of an ailing lord. She tended to the dying man's needs, soothing his spirit with words and making him a cross out of rushes that she'd found on the floor.

SYMBOL RITUAL

RITUAL FOR REJUVINATION

Draw upon the energy of this symbol to heal and restore your spirits. Brigid was a goddess of the hearth and fire, and this ritual uses this element in the form of a candle.

You will need: a pin, a white candle, a lighter or matches

- ∞ Take the pin and carve Brigid's cross into the candle wax – white candles are linked to purity and peace. This doesn't have to be perfect; a simple representation of the symbol will suffice. Take your time as you do this and think about the refreshing, healing energy of the deity associated with the symbol.
- ∞ When you've finished, position the candle safely on a table and light it. As you do this, think about Brigid's role as a fire goddess and how the burning flame has the power to cleanse and protect.
- ∞ Focus your attention on the candle and let your gaze soften. Enjoy watching the flame flicker and dance.
- ∞ Imagine that with every breath you take, your body and mind relaxes and you become lighter and brighter. All of the stress and tension that you have been carrying slips from your shoulders.
- ∞ Allow yourself this time to be still, and just focus on the light of the flame and the symbol of the cross.
- ∞ Let the candle burn down, or, when you're ready, carefully put it out.

MONTHLY SPELL

SPELL FOR GOOD FORTUNE AND TO ATTRACT BLESSINGS

The Celts regularly petitioned the deities for help, often using simple prayers, chants and poetic words, which were carried on the wind to attract their attention. This spell uses the power of words to draw opportunities for success and abundance.

You will need: a feather, a piece of paper and a pen

- ∞ Write your wish down so you know exactly what you want to say. Keep it simple, like, 'I wish for good fortune to change my day, may success and abundance come my way'.
- ∞ Practise saying this a few times so it is clear in your mind.
- ∞ Take the feather outside on a windy day.
- ∞ Hold it in both hands, spin around, and as you do, say your wish out loud. Then, release the feather into the breeze.
- ∞ Don't worry if it doesn't get carried away. Your words are powerful enough to spark positive change.

SPR

ING

As the sun peeks a sleep-wary head over the horizon, the brilliance of its rays stretches across the barren winter landscape. There's a stirring, prickling of excitement as the tribe gathers upon the highest hill. They look to the skies with radiant smiles while the hooded priests lift their faces in acknowledgement. Some raise their hands, arms outstretched in an embrace to an unseen god, for there is much thanks to be had here. The spring has at last returned. The earth bristles with the potential of new life and there is hope.

It is time for the land to be cleared, the soil prepared and seeds to be sown. It is time for calloused hands to dig deep and feel the replenishing moisture of the earth and plant for the future. Chants and prayers will be said to secure a healthy crop, and all will be well, for the Wheel of the Year keeps turning and the season's magic has something for everyone.

MARCH

CELTIC FOLKLORE

TREE NYMPHS

The Celts believed that everything upon the earth had a distinctive energy that could be tapped into. In particular, natural objects such as stones, rocks, plants and most prominently trees harboured a spiritual essence. The Druids, who were considered guides and spiritual teachers among the Celtic tribes, spent their time studying various elements of the natural world, learning how to harness the power of nature's gifts. They were fascinated by trees, and believed that each one had a spirit – a type of nymph that lived within the heart of the trunk, but could move freely in the forest. These beings were highly secretive and tended to avoid prying human eyes, but it's thought that the Druids learned how to commune with them and use their magic in rites and rituals.

Oak trees were thought to be the most common dwellings for tree nymphs. Sturdy and ancient, they often appeared in clusters, tucked away in the sprawling woodland. As such, they were the perfect hiding place for fairies. They were also considered close to the heavens, and the Druids soon sequestered these sacred spaces for their magical workings. Tree nymphs were synonymous with the moon, and were thought to emerge after dark to protect the forest from outsiders.

TREE OF THE MONTH

ALDER

Birth Sign Dates: 18 March - 14 April

An auspicious tree to the Celts, the alder was revered for its strength and resilience. Often seen growing by riverbanks, the wood of this tree appears even stronger when submerged in water, and when cut, changes colour from white to orangey-red. It was thought that this magical tree could help those lost in the Otherworld find their way back to reality. The size and stability of the tree made it the perfect refuge when under attack, which is why it's synonymous with protection. An ancient Irish legend states that the first man was made of alder wood.

Focused and ready for action, those born under this tree sign do not shy away from a challenge. These characters have an innate determination and like to shake things up. Gregarious and charming, they are confident souls who draw people in droves, but their sense of urgency means they often lack patience when dealing with others.

CELTIC DEITY

RHIANNON

This selfless deity is an example of purity, forgiveness and the gentle illumination of the moon. Depicted as a beautiful young woman with flowing golden robes and riding a powerful white stallion, Rhiannon is a Celtic horse goddess. It's thought she emerged from a fairy mound upon her trusty steed, only to grab the attention of the young Lord Pwyll of Dyfed. After chasing her for many days, they eventually met, fell in love and married. While this should have been a fairytale ending, especially after Rhiannon gave birth to their son, the story took an unexpected turn.

One night while she was resting and her handmaids had fallen asleep, the baby was kidnapped. Her maids, upon waking, knew they would in trouble for not watching over the child, so they slaughtered a young pup and smeared its blood over the infant's cot and onto Rhiannon's lips. Lord Pwyll was aghast at the news that his wife had slaughtered their child, but he could not bring himself to kill her. Instead, he chained her to the castle gatehouse, where she would carry visitors day and night to and from the castle upon her back. The penance was tough and Rhiannon was weary, but she accepted her fate with dignity. Many years later the truth was discovered, and the young boy was found alive. Rhiannon was swiftly exonerated and became a symbol of strength, grace and forgiveness.

DEITY RITUAL

RITUAL TO RELEASE THE PAST

Rhiannon knew the gentle glow of the moon's light would eventually reveal the truth and free her from purgatory. While most would have felt bitter under the circumstances, she embodied the softness of this mystical orb, and freed herself by letting go of any hurt.

You can do the same by harnessing the moon's light in this simple ritual to help you release the past and move forwards.

You will need to do this on an evening when the moon is in its crescent form, and getting smaller, known as waning. This moon phase is associated with 'letting go'.

∞ To begin, write a few words on a piece of paper to sum up what you would like to release. This could be a past hurt or fear, a situation or even a bad habit.

∞ Gates were associated with this goddess, so you will need to stand before a gate, holding the paper in both hands.

∞ Read through the paper as you stand beneath the light of the moon.

∞ Out loud or in your head, say, 'I release this that ties my heart. I move forward to a fresh start'.

∞ Open the gate, walk through and close it behind you.

∞ To finish, either tear the paper into lots of pieces or screw it up into a tiny ball and dispose of it in your recycling.

SACRED SITE

THE PRINCE OF GLAUBERG STATUE

Hesse, Germany

Cast in sandstone, this life-sized statue marked the burial mound of a Celtic prince. Dating back to around 500 BCE, the statue itself shows the warrior clad in a tunic with trousers, wearing a sword and shield. The halo-like headdress is thought to represent hair, which at the time would have been backcombed with tree sap and lime to appear more fearsome. While the statue now stands in the Keltenwelt am Glauberg, this was once the site of several Celtic burial mounds.

SYMBOL

DARA KNOT

Celtic knots come in all shapes and sizes, and these interlacing patterns are thought to represent the infinite connections that bind us together, and the ongoing cycle of life and death. The entwined curves that twist and turn to create unity are considered a positive omen and are synonymous with love and happiness.

The Dara knot is a symbol of strength and is imbued with the power of nature. It's thought this knot was based upon the vast, sprawling roots of the oak tree. The criss-cross pattern mimics the tangled roots, and the word Dara comes from the Irish word *doire*, meaning 'oak tree'. The Celts were particularly enamoured with this tree, and associated it with ancient wisdom. The roots, which anchored the trunk to the earth, were seen as the seat of this power, and the knot was thought to represent their resilience. As such, it was often carved into armour and weaponry.

SYMBOL RITUAL

RITUAL FOR RESILIENCE

Use the symbolism of the Dara knot to feel grounded and build resilience. The tangled pattern of the symbol will help you feel rooted to the earth.

You will need: an image of the Dara knot

- ∞ Familiarize yourself with the image of the Dara knot. Notice how the pattern intertwines like roots connected in a continual loop.
- ∞ Stand with your feet hip-width apart, shoulders relaxed.
- ∞ Tighten your core by pulling your stomach muscles in, and lengthen your spine.
- ∞ Take a long deep breath in through your nose, and as you do, imagine the air travelling up through the sole of each foot, into your chest.
- ∞ Hold the breath for a couple of counts and then release slowly through your mouth.
- ∞ As you exhale, imagine tiny roots unfurling from each foot and stretching beneath the ground. Picture these roots spreading underfoot, while remaining connected to each other.
- ∞ Continue to breathe in this way, visualizing the roots getting stronger and more interconnected.
- ∞ Feel the weight of your body anchored to the earth and know that you are supported.
- ∞ Sense the connection getting stronger, and imagine the energy of the earth imbuing you with resilience.

MONTHLY SPELL

SPELL TO CALM THE MIND AND BOOST PERSONAL POWER

The Celts believed in the importance of family ties, and this went beyond the grave, as they called upon their ancestors for advice and support. Take inspiration from this practice by connecting with loved ones and those who have passed on.

You will need: old family pictures (include deceased family members), a candle, a collection of crystals or stones, a lighter or matches

- ∞ Arrange the photographs in a large circle on a table. Leave some space in the centre to position the candle and crystals or stones.
- ∞ Arrange the crystals or stones around the candle, and then light it.
- ∞ Sit and gaze at each of the pictures. Linger over each one, and if you know or knew the relative, bring them to mind. Recall any positive memories that you have of this person. Recognize that you have ancestral ties with each person pictured, and that they are a part of your story.
- ∞ Acknowledge this by saying thank you for their presence in your life.
- ∞ To finish, say, 'I am imbued by your blessings, infused with your strength. I am calmed by your presence, and soothed by your love'.
- ∞ Blow the candle out and keep the pictures and crystals somewhere safe.

APRIL

CELTIC TRADITION

BARDS, OVATES AND DRUIDS

The Celts were organized when it came to their societal structure. Everyone had their place and role within the tribe. The Druids, who were the priests, magicians and advisors within the group, had their own structure, which was divided into three separate roles.

The first was the bards, a collection of creatives whose purpose was to record the history of the community through song, poem and story. These imaginative souls would make up magical chants and deliver potent lessons through the medium of storytelling.

The second, the ovates, were the nature lovers. They studied the world around them looking for signs and meaning. Connecting deeply with plants and animals, they uncovered the healing properties of certain herbs and put them to use in rituals and spells. They could divine the future and were gifted with prophetic visions.

The final division, and probably the most highly regarded, were the Druids. They were the astronomers and the moral philosophers who had the responsibility of maintaining some kind of law and order within the tribe. Any kind of dispute went to the Druids for consideration, and they were even involved in key decisions relating to war and battle manoeuvres. These learned men charted the passage of time and looked to the heavens for inspiration.

TREE OF THE MONTH

WILLOW

Birth Sign Dates: 15 April - 12 May

Known as the Tree of Enchantment, the willow was sacred to the Celts. Commonly seen straddling riverbanks, it marked the border between other realms, and was synonymous with healing, new growth and flexibility. To the Druids, it was especially important, and often appeared in their creation myths. In one tale, the willow stood guard over two scarlet eggs, keeping them safe from harm during the gestation period. When the eggs eventually hatched at the beginning of spring, one became the fiery orb of the sun, and the other, the earth. Bards would often carry a sprig from the willow tree for inspiration.

Those born under this tree sign usually have a poetic soul. They appreciate the subtle nuances of life and intuitively know things. Their innate wisdom comes from the ability to take a step back and perceive a situation from all sides. Highly creative, willow personalities are blessed with a vivid imagination and a need to express themselves.

CELTIC DEITY

LUGH

One of the most prominent Celtic deities, Lugh was the all-seeing god of the sun. Wise and spirited, he could control the elements, conjuring storms and bringing the gift of light and sunshine. A skilled warrior, he was often called Lugh Lámfada or Lámfhota, meaning 'of the long hand' or 'long armed', which referred to his spear-throwing ability. According to legend, it was Lugh who led the magical fairy race the Tuatha Dé Danann into war against the one-eyed giant Balor and his demonic seafaring race, the Fomorians. Using his powers, Lugh imbued all of their weapons with magic to give them a chance against such a formidable foe. The infamous Battle of Mag Tuired came to an end when Lugh launched his magical spear into the air, striking Balor swiftly and ending his life. A forty-year period of peace and abundance followed this victory.

A trickster god, Lugh could be wily at times and would often cheat or lie to get his own way. That said, he was still the god of oaths and justice, and was particularly revered by Celtic nobility, who would petition him for assistance in ruling.

DEITY RITUAL

RITUAL FOR ABUNDANCE

Lugh was a craftsman, happy to turn his hand to almost anything. He was admired for his artistic talents, and used them along with his natural dazzling energy to gain favour and create abundance.

Harness your own creative power by using your hands and the sun's vibrant light to create a magical wildflower meadow.

You will need: a patch of soil, a garden rake, a pack of wildflower seeds, a watering can, wire mesh (optional)

- ∞ Start by clearing a patch of soil ready to plant your seeds. Use the rake to sift through the area and remove any stones. This will also refresh the earth with nutrients as you stir up layers of soil.
- ∞ When you're happy that the area looks ready, begin to plant your seeds. Sprinkle them liberally over the soil.
- ∞ As you do this, imagine you're planting seeds for success, and lots of thoughts and ideas that will grow and become opportunities for you to create abundance.
- ∞ Fill the watering can and water the area well. You may want to cover the section with some wire mesh to keep the birds from picking off the seeds and to protect your future blooms from other pests while they become established.
- ∞ Monitor the area and water when needed.
- ∞ Enjoy watching the sun's light do its magic, as your seeds begin to grow into beautiful blooms that attract pollinators into your garden.

SACRED SITE

GRIANÁN OF AILEACH

County Donegal, Ireland

Also known as the Sun Palace, this ancient ringfort is situated on the Inishowen peninsula. Once a royal citadel between the 5th and 12th centuries, it was at the heart of one of the ancient kingdoms of Ulster belonging to the infamous O'Neill clan. Most likely built over a neolithic burial mound, it was used to perform rites and rituals and petition Celtic deities. Folklore attests that the town Cashel near the ringfort was created by the king of the magical Tuatha Dé Danann.

SYMBOL

THE TREE OF LIFE

A symbol of unity and strength, the Tree of Life, known as the *Crann Bethadh* in Irish, was an important symbol for the Celtic people. Trees were seen as silent sentinels imbued with energy and magical power. With their trailing roots and their network of branches, which spread to create a woodland canopy, they connected the air, earth and the Underworld.

The Celts noted the way they grew, and how the branches stretched to the heavens. They acknowledged the presence of the root system, which nurtured the tree, giving it strength and vitality. They also appreciated the cycles of life that were visible in their changing appearance as each season passed.

The Tree of Life symbol illustrates the connection we have to the natural world and to each other. The downward flowing roots and the branches, which surge upwards and are often enclosed within a circle, represent the cyclical nature of life, and depict a link to our ancestors in the spirit realm.

SYMBOL RITUAL

RITUAL TO RECHARGE AND BOOST ENERGY

To recharge and reconnect with the natural world, harness the power of your favourite tree. By engaging your senses in the presence of nature and being more mindful, you will feel instantly uplifted.

You will need: a tree of your choosing growing outside, perhaps in a park, nature reserve or the countryside

∞ Stand facing the tree and wrap your arms around the body of the trunk. Depending on how wide this is, you might not be able to reach around it fully.

∞ Press your cheek up to the bark of the tree and notice how it feels against your skin. Notice too how your hands feel against the rough grainy wood.

∞ Take a long slow breath in and engage your senses.

∞ Notice the earthy smell of the wood, and the freshness in the air. Notice how the tree supports your weight. Bring your attention to your feet and how they feel planted in the earth below.

∞ Exhale and release any tension. Imagine any tension being absorbed into the body of the tree.

∞ Stand for as long as you feel comfortable, breathing in the energy of the tree and letting it support you.

∞ To finish, sit beneath the branches and say a silent thank you to the tree for sharing its vitality with you.

∞ Bring to mind the Tree of Life symbol and know that whenever you need an energy boost you can picture it, and feel the sense of wonder that you just experienced.

MONTHLY SPELL

SPELL TO PROMOTE JOY AND ATTRACT POSITIVE ENERGY

The Celts revered the sun's brightness, believing the warmth and light to be a blessing. This was particularly true from spring through to summer, when they saw the effects of the sun's power upon their newly planted crops.

Harness this energy yourself with this simple spell that you can perform at the start of the day. This works especially well if you can perform it during sunrise.

You will need: a piece of paper, a pen, something gold (like jewellery, a bead, trinket or a gold-coloured coin)

- ∞ To begin, throw back the curtains or blinds, open the window and embrace the light of the morning sun.
- ∞ Stand before the window and say, 'I open my heart and mind, and let the positive energy of this radiant orb flow through me'.
- ∞ Next, write a wish for joy and positivity on the piece of paper, like, 'I wish to attract more positive energy, and to feel joyful today and every day'.
- ∞ Place the wish on a windowsill and place the gold object on top.
- ∞ Leave them there throughout the day and retrieve the following morning.
- ∞ Read your wish out loud once more and keep the gold object about your person as a magical charm to attract blessings.

MAY

CELTIC FESTIVAL

BALTANE

The Celts rejoiced at the coming of spring and the return of the light of the sun on the 1st May. The celebration known as Beltane, which comes from the Irish word *Bealtaine*, was one of four major fire festivals that marked the mid-quarter points of the Celtic calendar, the Wheel of the Year. Also called *Cétshamhain*, meaning 'first of summer', Beltane is halfway between the spring equinox and the summer solstice. It's the point when the seasons turn and the earth bristles with new life.

At this time, all fires within each home were extinguished and an enormous communal pyre was built in their place. The villagers would gather, feast and dance around this, while making pledges and petitions to the gods. A torch was then lit from the flames and passed between them to relight the hearth in each home. The idea was that the central fire brought each family closer together to create a sense of community after the harsh winter months. Cattle were also made to walk between two fires as they made their way to the fields in order to cleanse and purify them and ensure a healthy herd for the coming year. The theme of fertility was important at this time, and couples would leap hand-in-hand over the flames in the hope that they might be blessed with new life.

TREE OF THE MONTH

HAWTHORN

Birth Sign Dates: 13 May - 9 June

The pretty hawthorn tree flowers, at the threshold of summer, bring an abundance of pink and white blooms. To the Celts, this tree had a mixed reputation. It was thought to belong to the fairies, making it inherently magical. A sprig or fallen twig was often carried to ensure good luck, or given as a gift of love. But that said, it was also a bad omen to carry any part of the tree inside the home. Synonymous with protection and fertility, the tree played a key role in May Beltane celebrations.

There's an air of mystery to those born under this tree sign. Hawthorn characters have a rich inner world, which they conceal beneath a placid and calm exterior. Able to see the bigger picture, they make good confidantes, offering advice that is practical and non-judgemental. Naturally curious, the hawthorn personality also absorbs information and seeks to broaden their horizons at every opportunity.

CELTIC DEITY

ÁINE

Áine was the beautiful Celtic goddess of love, wealth and sovereignty. Synonymous with midsummer and the generous light of the sun, some tales associated with her were brutal and hinted at the harshness of life, particularly for Celtic women. The daughter of Eogabail, a key member of the magical Tuatha Dé Danann, she had many attributes. Some said she was fairy queen, while others believed she represented a lighter side of the triple goddess Morrigan. Usually depicted with a sun disc above her head and almost always riding a vibrant red mare, Áine was a radiant beauty who captured many hearts. Indeed, it's thought she was responsible for teaching humans the meaning of true love.

According to one tale, Áine went out riding one day and encountered the mythical king of Munster, Ailill Aulom. Selfish at heart and with a cruel streak, he decided there and then that he must have her. When Áine refused his advances, he raped her. But this was not the end of the tale. In retaliation, the goddess bit off his ear, an act that would dethrone him, for only those 'unblemished' were fit to wear the crown. With this one deed she became a symbol of hope to many Celtic women who had suffered hardship and a similar fate while protecting their homestead.

DEITY RITUAL

RITUAL FOR SELF-LOVE

Áine was linked to fairy magic, being born from the magical Tuatha Dé Danann. It's thought she literally shone like the sun and moon, emanating a radiant glow wherever she went. It's no wonder so many of her followers wanted to be in her presence!

Turn up your own shine with a self-love ritual inspired by this deity.

∞ Stand beneath the light of the sun (outside if possible) so that you can feel the warming rays upon your skin.

∞ Take a long slow breath in and place your hands on the space just above your naval. Feel the warmth of your palms in this place.

∞ Imagine there's a thermostat dial beneath your fingers, which controls the brightness of your aura, the field of light and energy around your body.

∞ As you exhale, imagine turning the thermostat up so that your aura shines brighter.

∞ For every breath you take, imagine being infused with the light of the sun, and as you exhale, feel that energy growing as your aura sparkles.

∞ Continue to breathe in this way for a couple of minutes.

∞ To finish, say out loud or in your head, 'I am filled with light and love'.

SACRED SITE

THE SOURCE OF THE SEINE

Le Plateau de Langres, France

Located in Côte-d'Or in a listed area bought by the City of Paris in 1864, there sits a romantic grotto, which marks the source of the Seine. It was considered sacred by the Celts, who believed that any place where water sprang forth and joined together was a boundary between the physical and spiritual worlds. Today, a white stone water nymph languishes in this spot as a reminder of the river that once flowed and the Gallo-Roman sanctuary that was considered a powerful source of healing by visiting pilgrims.

SYMBOL

TRISKELION

The triskelion, also called the triskele and the triple spiral, is an ancient symbol used by the Celts from 500 BCE onwards. The three interlocking spirals that form the body of this symbol are the key to deciphering its potency. The Celts believed that good things came in threes, taking their lead from Mother Nature and looking at the land, sea and sky as a triple unit. They began to identify other significant groups of three such as the three aspects of their Triple Goddess: the maiden, mother and crone. The triskelion became a representation of the power of three, and was synonymous with the cycle of life, death and rebirth.

Carved into artefacts, weapons and burial mounds, it was an important motif that united body, mind and spirit, and also signified strength and the ability to go with the flow.

SYMBOL RITUAL

RITUAL TO DEAL WITH STRESS

Tune into the fluid nature of the triskelion with a simple doodling exercise that will help you release tension and embrace the ebb and flow of life. Working with the continuous pattern of this symbol will help to still the mind.

You will need: a clear, fairly large image of the triskelion, a pencil, a piece of paper

- ∞ Spend a few minutes acclimatizing yourself with the symbol.
- ∞ When you're ready, take the pencil and trace over the image of the symbol a few times so that you can feel the flow of the spirals.
- ∞ Next, take a fresh piece of paper, and either trace over the symbol if you can see it through the paper, or try to draw it freehand. This doesn't have to be exact; a representation that captures the three connected spirals will suffice. Let your eyes relax, breathe deeply and do this in a continuous flow until it almost becomes second nature.
- ∞ See this as a doodling exercise, and relax your body and mind as you trace or recreate the image. Let any thoughts flow into and out of your mind and simply bring your attention back to the doodle. The combination of mindful focus and repetitive action should help you release stress and centre your body and mind.

MONTHLY SPELL

SPELL TO PROMOTE NEW GROWTH IN ANY AREA OF LIFE

The Celts believed in fairies and nature spirits, and would petition these playful beings for help. Hillside mounds, valleys and tree-lined lakes were just some of the special places that were recognized as crossover points to the fairy Otherworld, and the Celts would leave food, gifts and other trinkets in the hope they'd be exchanged for a fey blessing.

Take inspiration from this and find a magical spot in nature where you can visualize new growth, and make your dreams come true.

You will need: a small bag of sunflower seeds

- ∞ Find somewhere that you enjoy walking in nature. This could be a spot in the countryside, a local park or even your garden. The Celts were fond of hill mounds, shady spaces beneath trees or by free-flowing water, so if you can find somewhere like this, even better.
- ∞ Once you've located the ideal space, take your sunflower seeds and sprinkle them in a wide circle on the ground.
- ∞ Step into the centre of the circle and sit down.
- ∞ Place your hands either side of you so that you can feel the earth and the grass between your fingers.
- ∞ Focus on the area of life where you'd like to see growth. Picture what this might look like in your mind. For example, if you're looking for love, you might see growth as you go out on a romantic date.
- ∞ Close your eyes and say, 'As I see so may it be'.

SUM

MER

Summer sweeps gallantly over the land, its skirts adorned with meadows of wildflowers and sweet-smelling herbs. It's a welcome visitor, and like any esteemed guest, the people make summer feel at home by lighting a fire, a symbol of the light it brings to the earth. They sing songs and regale tales of the greatness of the gods who keep the seasonal wheel rolling. Then, they make their petitions, sacrificing what they can to secure a bountiful harvest, for this is a time of celebration.

Summer's generosity knows no bounds. It offers abundance freely with its life-giving warmth. Every man, woman and child feels the brightness. Every creature and blade of grass feels the benefit of summer's arrival. It's time to relax, to trust in the power of the nature and dance in summer's nurturing heat.

JUNE

CELTIC TRADITION

DIVINATION TECHNIQUES

The Druids turned to nature to divine the future, an act known as divination. Looking for signs using plants and animal entrails, they also studied the skies, looking at the movement of the stars and making connections between them. One of their favourite forms of prediction involved reading the clouds, a practice known as neldoracht. They would use their intuition to decipher shapes and symbols, which would help them foretell future events. While this might sound simple, they often wrapped themselves in the hide of a bull to conceal their clairvoyance and aid their success, a tradition known as the Tarbh Feis.

Birds too were a source of inspiration. Their ability to live on the land but also soar towards the heavens gave them spiritual significance. They were seen as messengers from the gods, and held potent magic. The Druids would watch them take to the air and study the direction and speed of their flight for insights into the future.

The tribal fire, being one of the four elements, was also used for scrying. The shapes seen dancing within the flames provided wisdom and often determined future actions, while free-flowing bodies of waters such as lakes, streams and rivers were also used as scrying tools.

TREE OF THE MONTH

OAK

Birth Sign Dates: 10 June - 7 July

The oak tree was held in high regard by the Celts. Its sturdy branches reached to the heavens, while its sprawling roots anchored the trunk to the earth, making it a bridge between worlds and a way of accessing other realms. The word Druid comes from the Celtic world for the oak tree, *duir*, and reveals some of its significance. Indeed, the priests of each tribe would study and perform their rites and rituals within oak groves to enhance their success. It was thought that eating the fruit of the tree, the humble acorn, could imbue a person with the wisdom of the gods.

As you might expect from those born under this tree sign, strength and fortitude are at the heart of their character. These individuals do not give up easily and have the ability to achieve great things. Nurturing and generous in their attitude to others, oak personalities will do their best to help in any situation. Their protective nature also means they always like to be in control.

CELTIC DEITY

THE DAGDA

Father of all, the Dagda was considered one of the most powerful gods of the Celtic pantheon. Like many other deities, he belonged to the magical race of the Tuatha Dé Danann. A leader and a king, he was imbued with supernatural strength and had many other attributes.

While he was usually depicted as an older, bearded warrior, he was most commonly petitioned for his magical ability and innate knowledge. The Dagda carried an enchanted harp with him, which inspired courage, soothed the mind and could play by itself. He wielded a club that could both kill and restore life, and his cauldron – a great bottomless pit that provided sustenance and strength – was never empty. In addition, he always had two pigs: one that was forever roasting on the spit, and another that he kept by his side. His orchard was full of fruit at any time of year, another symbol of his abundant spirit.

The Dagda could secure wealth and a good crop if appeased with the right gifts. Also known as the good god because of his benevolent nature, he wed the goddess known as the Morrigan in a union that brought the powers of light and dark together.

DEITY RITUAL

RITUAL TO ATTRACT PROSPERITY

The Dagda was generous and associated with wealth. He could be called upon to boost abundance, and his cauldron, which was forever full like his orchard, was an emblem of affluence and prosperity.

Tap into this deity's energy by connecting with two of his most potent symbols.

You will need: a large bowl (preferably one that you are drawn to or that looks attractive), a small piece or paper or a Post-it note, a pen, your favourite fruits

∞ Position the bowl in the centre of the table where you eat. This represents the Dagda's cauldron, and the place where you nourish your body and mind, which in turn boosts vitality.

∞ Take a small piece of paper or a Post-it note and write, 'I am blessed with the rich flow of abundance from the universe'.

∞ Place this in the bowl and then cover it with some of your favourite fruits, which represent the Dagda's orchard.

∞ Choose a fruit to eat every day, and give thanks each time for this gift. Always ensure the bowl is full of fresh ripe fruit by constantly replenishing what you eat.

SACRED SITE

BRÚ NA BÓINNE

County Meath, Ireland

Located within a bend on the River Boyne stands an ancient complex of monuments crafted from earth and stone. Also known as the Boyne Valley tombs, this is the largest and oldest collection of megalithic art in Europe, being in existence for over five thousand years. The structures, which are comprised of three main sites – Newgrange, Knowth and Dowth – were built as homes and used as ceremonial spaces. Celtic tribes would gather in each of these sacred spots to worship the sun and moon and chart the movement of the stars.

SYMBOL

THE AILM

One of the oldest Celtic motifs thought to date back to the 1st century BCE, the ailm symbol is synonymous with strength, endurance and purity. While many other symbols include intricate knotwork, the ailm symbol embodies the simplicity of nature. It features a small cross encased within a circle, a representation of the innate strength of the soul that arises when a person is challenged.

The ailm symbol is often associated with the pine tree, which covered much of the landscape at that time. This lofty fir was linked to resilience and healing, attributes that the symbol also adopted. The ailm is based upon the letter A in the Celtic Ogham alphabet, a primitive form of communication comprised of twenty letters, which were carved into stone monoliths and burial chambers. Originally, the ailm symbol was a simple cross, but over the years the circle was added.

SYMBOL RITUAL

RITUAL FOR CALM

Harness your innate strength with this easy ritual, which draws upon the properties of this symbol and instils a sense of calm. When combined with an easy breathing technique the ailm promotes peaceful energy.

You will need: an image of the ailm symbol, a tall white candle, a pin, a candleholder, a lighter or matches

∞ To begin, familiarize yourself with the symbol.

∞ Take the white candle and, using the pin, carefully carve the ailm symbol into the wax. If you have room you could do this on both sides of the candle, depending on how wide it is. The candle has peaceful properties and represents the pine tree.

∞ Place the candle safely on a candleholder and light it. Then sit back and watch as the flame begins to grow.

∞ Draw a long, deep breath in. Imagine you are pulling the air through your feet, up your legs and into your chest. Sit with the breath here and imagine a flame bursting to life inside you.

∞ Exhale slowly through your lips and imagine the flame travelling up through your throat and out of your mouth.

∞ Continue to breathe in this way for five to ten minutes, drawing the energy within, and then releasing it into the world.

∞ As you do this, gaze at the flame and the symbol on the candle and think about what it represents.

∞ Extinguish the candle when you're ready, so that you can use it again each time you perform this ritual.

MONTHLY SPELL

SPELL TO CENTRE YOURSELF AND CREATE BALANCE

The elements of earth, air, fire and water were important to the Celts. They were especially significant in rituals to establish balance and create unity. Gifts that embraced the qualities of each element were combined to manifest harmony and equilibrium.

This simple spell will help you connect with all of the elements and create more balance in your life.

You will need: a stone (to represent earth), a feather (to represent air), a tealight (to represent fire), a lighter or matches, a small cup of water (to represent water)

- ∞ To begin, place the stone in front of you and say, 'I am born of the earth.'
- ∞ Next, take the feather and gently drop it to rest by the stone. Say, 'I breathe of the air'.
- ∞ Place the tealight next to the stone and feather and light it. Say, 'I ignite the fire within'.
- ∞ Finally, dip your fingers in the cup of water and sprinkle it over the stone, the feather and the tealight. Say, 'I am refreshed with water'.
- ∞ To finish, sit and consider all the elements and the role they play in your life, and say, 'I embrace all of the elements. I am in perfect balance with myself and the world around me'.

JULY

CELTIC TRADITION

THE OTHERWORLD

Described as a mystical place where the deities lived, the Celtic Otherworld had many names. Some tribes believed it was a fairy realm filled with magical beings, while others preferred to think of it as a mirror world to the earth, and a place that could be reached at certain times of the year such as Beltane and Samhain, when the veil between life and death was thin.

Welsh tribes called it Annwn, a place of many realms and islands, while to the Irish it was Tír na nÓg, meaning 'The Land of Youth'. Synonymous with eternal youth and beauty, it was thought that those who lived in the Otherworld would never age or die. Instead, they lived an enchanted life filled with joy and love. It's no wonder that it was referred to as the Delightful Plain, the Land of the Living, or the Land of the Young.

While many found themselves in the Otherworld after falling prey to fairy trickery or stumbling upon a magical mound, others actively sought out a route where they would cross sacred water or be led astray by a beautiful being upon a glass boat. While a visit to the Otherworld was always blessed with the gift of sacred knowledge, when a lost soul returned, they would find that a hundred years or more had passed, and that their loved ones were no longer on the earthly plain.

TREE OF THE MONTH

HOLLY

Birth Sign Dates: 8 July - 4 August

Associated with peace and goodwill, the holly was sacred to the Druids, who revered its evergreen nature. They believed it remained verdantly green through the winter months to retain strength and keep the earth bountiful until the return of spring. A sign of the waning sun and the beginning of the summer solstice, the holly was resistant to lightning, and as such became a powerful symbol of protection. It was linked to the god of thunder Taranis, and often planted near dwellings to shield them from harm.

Highly intelligent, those born under the holly sign can thrive in any environment. These characters have a tactful and inspiring way with words. Their competitive nature means they almost always come out on top, and will often hold positions of power. People naturally look up to this sign and rely on them for guidance and leadership.

CELTIC DEITY

CERNUNNOS

Deep in the heart of the forest, the Lord of the Wild Things lives. With a swarthy appearance and an antlered brow, he blends well with the flora and fauna that he is sworn to protect. Cernunnos is the name of this Celtic god, and he has ancient roots. From crudely daubed cave paintings to carvings on the silver vessel the Gundestrup Cauldron – discovered in Denmark and thought to be dated around the 1st century BCE – this god has existed in one form or another for thousands of years. Often depicted with a stag at his side or sitting cross-legged among plants and tree roots, the Horned God, as he is also known, is an aspect of the forest. He is also a spiritual guardian who is linked to the Green Man, a leafy representation of the spirit of the woods.

Thought to be the god of the hunt, Cernunnos represents the old ways of being and doing, living in harmony with the land and all of the wild creatures. It's believed that his horns were borrowed by the Christian faith to create the demonic appearance of Satan. The Celts revered this god and his feral ways, and celebrated his presence by dressing in animal skins and feathers. They would dance around fires, adorned in their skulls and bones to harness his power.

DEITY RITUAL

RITUAL TO GENERATE NEW WEALTH

Cernunnos is also associated with wealth and often depicted carrying a purse full of coins, or a bag of grain. In this guise, he can help you nurture opportunities for abundance, while also connecting you with the uplifting power of nature.

Create more prosperity by sharing and showing your love to the natural world.

You will need: a piece of paper, a pen, a garden or outdoor window space, a handful of grain

- ∞ You're going to make your garden or outdoor window space a place where the wild things can thrive. To begin, make a list of things you can do to help all the creatures that visit this space. Here are some ideas to inspire you:
    - ∞ If you get birds in your garden, put up a feeder and make sure they have a water station and a bird box.
    - ∞ Pollinators such as bees and butterflies love wildflowers, so if you haven't already, you could create a wildflower meadow, or a couple of planters filled with their favourite blooms.
    - ∞ Leave a pile of compost, leaves and wood at the end of your garden for bugs and other invertebrates to take shelter, and if you have the space, invest in a bee box.
- ∞ Once you have made as many improvements as you can, stand outside with a handful of grain or breadcrumbs for the birds, and say, 'I sow the seeds, I reap the rewards, I nurture nature to open new doors'.
- ∞ Sprinkle the crumbs upon the grass to finish.

SACRED SITE

THE DANUBE RIVER

Europe

The second longest river in Europe was of prime importance to the Celts. A source of sustenance and travel, the waters were considered sacred and named after the mother goddess Danu. Celtic tribes from the 3rd century BCE set up home along the river and swiftly spread, following its path through Europe towards the Black Sea. They believed that the goddess used the waters to open up the landscape for their occupation. While there is no specific worship site, the river in its entirety is considered a Celtic stronghold.

SYMBOL

THE SINGLE SPIRAL

The single spiral stands on its own and represents the radiance of the cosmos. The circular pattern relates to the cyclical nature of life and the interconnectedness of the universe. Every action has a reaction, and the Celts celebrated this connection to create a sense of belonging and unity. In particular, the anticlockwise spiral highlights the personal journey from the outer to the inner self, and the voyage of discovery that this takes. Often etched into stones and tree trunks or carved into jewellery, the single spiral is a reminder that growth and change are an important part of life.

SYMBOL RITUAL

RITUAL FOR DISCOVERY

Kickstart your journey of self-discovery with this ritual, which uses the single spiral as a meditation tool. This exercise will help you be in the present moment and enjoy a moment of calm.

You will need: an image of the single spiral

- ∞ Find a quiet place to sit. Make sure your back is supported by cushions and that you feel warm and relaxed.
- ∞ Acquaint yourself with the symbol by tracing your finger over the pattern from the inside out.
- ∞ Close your eyes and focus on your breathing. Note the journey of each breath as you inhale slowly, and then exhale. Take a few deep breaths to still your mind.
- ∞ Place your dominant hand over the centre of your chest. This is where your heart chakra – the energy centre that relates to your emotions – resides.
- ∞ With your index finger, slowly begin to recreate the single spiral in a continuous loop, going over the area a few times. As you do this, think about the cyclical nature of this motif, and how it leads you on a journey of self-discovery.
- ∞ Place your hand over this spot and feel the warmth as you breathe. Ask yourself: what do I need to learn right now? What guidance do I need? Let the answers come to you in their own time. Don't worry if your mind is empty. Simply relax, breathe and enjoy a moment of stillness. Inspiration comes with practice and allowing your mind time to regularly disengage in this way.
- ∞ When you're ready to finish, open your eyes and stretch your limbs.

MONTHLY SPELL

SPELL TO CONNECT WITH YOUR ANIMAL FRIENDS

The Celts embraced all the creatures of the earth. They understood the balance between life and death, and showed care and respect to the animals that they hunted. They also sought to commune with creatures such as bears, wolves, horses and stags in the hope of harnessing their powers.

Connect with the animals in your life with this simple spell to improve the flow of love and understanding between you.

You will need: a photo of the animal (this could be a pet) or a bird that visits your garden, a piece of quartz

- ∞ Sit with the photo in front of you and hold the quartz crystal in both hands. This crystal amplifies thoughts and feelings.
- ∞ Look at the creature and give thanks for its presence in your life.
- ∞ Think about all the qualities and things that you love about it. Let your emotions rise to the surface.
- ∞ Say, 'We are connected, we are as one. The bond we share is true and strong'.
- ∞ Place the crystal on the photo and leave it there overnight.
- ∞ Retrieve the photo in the morning and keep the crystal with you as a charm to attract your animal friend.

AUGUST

CELTIC TRADITION

LUGHNASADH

Also known as Lammas, Lughnasadh is an Irish Gaelic word which means 'Commemoration of Lugh.' An important fire festival to the Celts, it marked the first harvest upon the Wheel of the Year, when the fruits of all previous labours could be enjoyed. Celebrated on and around the 1st of August, it took its name from the renowned god of the sun and light Lugh, a warrior and king of the Tuatha Dé Danann.

A time of great community, clans would gather and feast upon an array of fruit, vegetables and freshly baked breads. Much merriment was had at this time, and there were often games and physical feats to demonstrate strength and dexterity, including wrestling and horse racing. These all took place in honour of Lugh, and as a way of bringing families together. Woven items and jewellery were displayed and given as gifts, and to cement loving bonds.

A central bonfire was lit and became the focal point for rites and rituals, which included offering gifts of grain to the gods to secure further prosperity and fertility throughout the year. Breads and baked goods were left or thrown into the flames, along with other ceremonial items, and the dancing around the fire was a popular activity.

TREE OF THE MONTH

HAZEL

Birth Sign Dates: 8 August – 1 September

The mystical hazel tree was held in high regard by the Celts and had a number of practical uses. The stakes were twisted into shape and utilized as building materials, and any fork-shaped twigs were used as divining tools to find water. Originally thought to reside in the Otherworld, the fruits of this tree were thought to be steeped in magical knowledge. When the purple nuts dropped into the water it was thought that ripples of inspiration appeared upon the surface. The Old English word *haesl* means 'rod of power', a nod towards the Druids who favoured the wood of this tree to make their beautifully carved staffs.

Organized and analytical, the hazel personality picks up on the finer details and always ensures everything is in place. While that might seem pedantic, these characters like to be well-informed and ready for every eventuality. With a head for business and an open mind, this tree sign loves to be active and learn new things.

CELTIC DEITY

SULIS

Sitting proud among the clouds, Sulis is the blinding eye of the sun. A radiant being that exudes warmth and healing energy, her name comes from the Proto-Celtic word for the sun, *sule*, while also overlapping with the old Irish word *súil*, meaning 'eye'. This gives her dual significance, as not only is she the all-seeing eye in the sky and often linked to prophecy, but she is also known as the Bright One.

With a beautiful halo of golden-red hair, which represents the many rays of the sun's light, Sulis was primarily the goddess of healing springs, and was associated with wells and waterways. Worship of this goddess spread quickly from Britain to as far as Hesse in Germany, where she was revered for her healing properties. The Celts built many shrines to her, but the most famous is located in Bath, England. Pilgrims travelled for miles to visit these magical waters and experience the healing touch of Sulis upon their skin. And, with the Roman invasion, Sulis transmuted into something new: she became a new goddess, which combined the Celtic deity Sulis with the Roman goddess of wisdom Minerva. In this guise, she was known as Aquae Sulis or Sulis-Minerva, a Gaulish interpretation of the original sun goddess, who was also synonymous with agriculture and the pledging of oaths.

DEITY RITUAL

RITUAL FOR SELF-HEALING

Sulis was renowned for her generosity and the blessings she endowed upon her followers. A benevolent being, the natural flow of her waters represented her giving nature, while the warmth of the sun highlighted the positive energy that emanated from those healing springs.

Embrace positivity with this self-healing ritual, which should leave you relaxed and revitalized.

You will need: a bowl of cold water, ice cube moulds, a handkerchief or muslin cloth, sunscreen

∞ Leave a bowl of cold tap water outside beneath the light of the midday sun. Let the water absorb the boundless heat of the healing rays.

∞ When the sun has set, bring the bowl inside.

∞ Decant the water into ice cube moulds. As you do this, think about the powerful healing energy of the sun, and how it radiates warmth and light every day.

∞ Put the moulds in your freezer overnight.

∞ The next day, retrieve one or two of the ice cubes and wrap them in a handkerchief or muslin cloth.

∞ Stand, sit or lay beneath the sun, making sure you are protected with sunscreen if needed, and rub the icy cloth over your head, neck, chest and other parts of your body.

∞ Enjoy the soothing sensation as the ice cools your skin. Breathe deeply and feel the warmth of the sun envelope you. Relax and enjoy a moment of stillness.

∞ To finish, let the ice melt.

SACRED SITE

MADRON WELL

Cornwall, England

Nestled to the north of the village of Madron sits Madron Well. Defined by a rough circle of granite stones, which were re-laid in the 1980s, the well is a sacred hotspot and was once a key part of Celtic worship. Its magical waters were thought to heal the sick and crippled when they entered the water three times. Pilgrims were also urged to tie a piece of clothing to a nearby tree, and as the rag deteriorated, so too would any affliction. Popular during Beltane celebrations, the well was renamed the Holy Well of St Madron by the Christians who also built a small chapel nearby.

SYMBOL

THE MOTHERHOOD KNOT

Family units were important to the Celts, and the strongest bond of all was that of a mother and her child. Knotwork was used in a variety of forms to show the connection between things in both the physical and spiritual realms. It was a way of depicting the interconnectedness of all the creatures upon the earth. The motherhood knot, also known as the mother's knot, is based upon a mother and child's embrace, where the continual looping resembles two hearts, with one lower than the other. It signifies the infinite and unbreakable bond between mother and child.

SYMBOL RITUAL

RITUAL FOR GRATITUDE

Strengthen your connections with others with a gratitude ritual based upon the motherhood knot. Taking inspiration from the original symbol, this exercise highlights your relationships with others, and helps you strengthen these bonds.

You will need: a piece of paper, a pen

- ∞ Draw a circle in the centre of the page to represent yourself.
- ∞ Now think about someone who is important to you. This could be your mother, another relative or a close friend. Draw a circle above yours that overlaps into your circle to represent your two hearts connecting. This doesn't have to be the same as the motherhood knot. It is just a representation of the symbol.
- ∞ Now think about all the things that this person does for you, and all of the wonderful qualities they bring to your life. You might want to jot these down somewhere on the page.
- ∞ Think about some things that you could do for them to show your gratitude, like giving them a quick call to see how they are, visiting them with flowers or cooking a lovely meal that you can share together. Write your ideas within the two circles.
- ∞ Commit to doing at least one of the things you have noted down over the next few days to show you care, and to cement the knot between you.

MONTHLY SPELL

SPELL FOR PEACE AND HEALING

Leaving votives in the form of jewellery, pieces of metal or even clothing was a popular pastime of the Celts, and a way of securing favour with the gods and connecting with the natural world. Many archaeological finds of this nature have been excavated from riverbeds and other bodies of water.

Make a wish for healing, either for yourself, someone in your life or for the world in general, with this simple spell inspired by this Celtic practice.

You will need: a length of ribbon or wool taken from a piece of your clothing, a white flower, access to free-flowing water

∞ Tie the ribbon or wool around the flower head to create your votive.

∞ As you do this, state your intention to heal out loud. For example, 'I wish for healing for [myself/my friend/the world]'.

∞ Take the votive to the body of water and gently drop it in, repeating your wish out loud as you do this.

∞ Watch as the votive is carried away by the flow of the water.

AUT

UMN

Autumn comes and with it, another cycle of the Wheel of the Year is completed. This is a time of dialling down that brings many pleasures. The light of the sun still lingers, but there is a gentle veil that settles upon the earth and a stillness, which offers respite. Now is the time to reap the rewards of spring's efforts. As the farmers gather in the fields, they evaluate the fruits of their labour, keenly assessing what they need to sustain them through the darker winter months. Together they work the land, harvesting what they can and returning with arms laden and weary.

The autumn equinox brings balance in all things and a bounty of goodies that leaves family tables groaning from the weight of success. The veil between worlds thins, the light dims and the communal fire is lit once more as a beacon for lost souls should they wish to return home for one final visit with their loved ones at Samhain.

SEPTEMBER

CELTIC MYTH

THE SALMON OF KNOWLEDGE

A popular Celtic myth about the Salmon of Knowledge has many variations, but the ending and lesson remain the same: while wisdom can be sought, it is never easily won, and sometimes comes with an unexpected twist.

In the beginning when the world was made, a solitary hazel tree stood guard over the Well of Wisdom. This tree was imbued with all of the knowledge of the Universe, and its fruit, when eaten, could pass on this special gift. A great speckled salmon lived within the well, and one day as the fruit fell from the tree into the well, it fed upon this treasure, becoming the Salmon of Knowledge.

A poet and druid named Finnegas tried to catch the salmon for years, but had no luck. One day, while fishing with his young apprentice Fionn, he managed to hook the fish and pull it to shore. Thrilled that he had finally won his prize he asked the boy to cook it on the fire while he went in search of more wood.

'Do not be tempted to eat any!' he warned, for he wanted all the knowledge for himself.

Fionn was a good boy and paid heed to this instruction, but while turning the fish on the embers, his thumb grazed the flesh and the flame. He cried out in pain and sucked at the burn. And in doing so, the wisdom of the world became his.

TREE OF THE MONTH

THE VINE

Birth Sign Dates: 2 September - 29 September

The vine was considered a tree by the Celts because of its swarthy trunk. Unlike some other plants, which needed no intervention to thrive, the vine was cultivated in the cool Celtic climate and encouraged to bear fruit. The intertwining nature of the vine meant it was associated with connection, emotional maturity and sacred knowledge. Despite the care that those early farmers had to give to the plant, it was surprisingly hardy and would often spring up in hard-to-reach areas, making it synonymous with tenacity.

Those born under the vine tree sign are a bundle of contradictions, and changeable characters that can be erratic at times and level-headed at others. This personality has the ability to be objective, but finds it hard to make decisions. Imbued with charm and elegance, vine signs have a flair for style and beauty and are often drawn to the arts.

CELTIC DEITY

AENGUS ÓG

As the wheel of the earth turned and spring flowed into summer, the Dagda, the father of all the Celtic pantheon, decided he needed a son as a representation of the vibrance of youth and beauty at his side. Being an almighty creator god, he cast a spell so that his son was conceived and birthed upon the same day. His son's name was Aengus, meaning 'chosen one', while Óg referred to his everlasting youth.

A handsome and loving god, Aengus had the gift of words and was synonymous with poetry, love, youthfulness and summer. Like his father, he could shapeshift, and also had the ability to resurrect the dead with his breath. Wherever he went a cluster of tweeting songbirds encircled his head. These feathered beauties were a symbolic representation of his kisses, which he would send in every direction. Being a romantic soul, Aengus pined for love and was visited nightly in his dreams by a beautiful maiden. So enamoured was he that he scoured the earth with the help of his magical kin to find this girl. Finally arriving at the shore of a lake known as the Dragon's Mouth, he found his love chained up with 150 other women. He outwitted their captor by changing all those present into swans, before shapeshifting into this elegant bird himself, calling out to his love. Once reunited, they flew away together.

DEITY RITUAL

RITUAL FOR NEW LOVE

Aengus was primarily associated with love, and birds of any kind were linked to this deity. His poetic way with words helped him woo the ladies and charm anyone he came into contact with. Channelling the gifts of this god can help you attract new love and boost your natural allure.

Use your words and nature's gifts to generate loving energy by creating a simple charm.

You will need: a bird's feather (a white feather is ideal as it symbolizes purity), a dish, a pink candle, a lighter or matches

∞ Place the feather on a dish in front of a pink candle. Pink is synonymous with love and beauty.

∞ Light the candle and spend a few minutes gazing at the bright flame.

∞ Breathe deeply and place your hands upon your heart.

∞ Say, 'My heart is open, my heart is light. My heart radiates loving energy that shines so bright'.

∞ Let the candle burn down naturally, then take the feather and keep it on your bedside table or beneath your pillow.

∞ Every evening before you go to sleep, hold the feather in both hands and repeat, 'My heart is open, my heart is light. My heart radiates loving energy that shines so bright'.

SACRED SITE

GAER FAWR

Powys, Wales

This ancient hillfort, just a few minutes away from the village of Guilsford, is obscured at first by thick woodland. Mostly filled with bluebells during the spring, you scale the steep bank to discover the heart of this site: a tree-dense plateau that still exhibits a sense of Celtic otherworldliness. The name Gaer Fawr means 'great fort' in Welsh, and demonstrates the size and importance of this place to those early tribes. Now, this forested mound protrudes like a thumb reaching for the sky, making it easy for tourists to find.

SYMBOL

THE TRIQUETRA

Also known as the trinity knot, the triquetra is based upon a triangular structure, with three interlacing arcs. Taken from the Latin word *triquetra*, meaning 'three cornered', this popular symbol was commonly seen on buildings or carved into Celtic crosses. It also made a prominent appearance in the infamous *Book of Kells*, a religious manuscript dating back to the medieval period. The continuous, everlasting flow of the symbol represents eternity, while the three arcs are a nod to the importance of the number three to the Celts. In particular, this symbol signified life, death and rebirth.

SYMBOL RITUAL

RITUAL FOR PERSONAL POWER

The triquetra can be used to boost personal power and unify different aspects of your personality when used in meditation, which uses the symbol combined with a potent visualization technique.

You will need: an image of the triquetra symbol, three stones

∞ Sit comfortably on the floor and position the stones in a triangular shape around you to represent the triquetra. Place one in front of you, and two at either side behind you.

∞ Look at the image of the symbol and when you're ready, close your eyes and bring the symbol to mind.

∞ Think of each arc as a quality, strength or aspect of your personality that empowers you. For example, you might have 'determination' as the first arc in front of you, 'honesty' as the second arc to the left and 'compassion' as the third arc to the right of you.

∞ As you inhale, visualize the arcs combining to create your own personal triangle of power.

∞ As you breathe out, feel the power of these three attributes filling you with light and energy.

∞ Continue to breathe in this way and know that each breath makes you stronger, brighter and more unified.

∞ When you're ready, open your eyes, give your body a shake and slowly step out of the triangle of power that you have created.

MONTHLY SPELL

SPELL TO BOOST INSIGHT AND INCREASE INTUITION

While the Druids were the spiritual priests and guides within the tribe, the gift of psychic perception wasn't just reserved for them. Most members of the tribe would have consulted the stars and looked to their surroundings for insights and omens.

Boost your intuitive skills by looking to the skies for inspiration with this simple spell.

You will need: a piece of moonstone

- ∞ Sit outside somewhere that you can see the patterns of the stars. Make sure you are comfortable and acclimatized with your surroundings.
- ∞ Hold the moonstone (a crystal that promotes psychic awareness) and spend a few minutes breathing deeply to focus your mind.
- ∞ Say, 'I welcome the elements, I welcome the night. I welcome my instincts to shine a light'.
- ∞ Place the moonstone on the ground and then say, 'I make a wish upon this night for clear vision and true insight'.
- ∞ Gaze up at the moon and the stars and let your eyes soften instead of focusing on a specific pattern. Relax and let your thoughts come and go.
- ∞ When you're ready, retrieve the moonstone and place it on your bedside table.
- ∞ Repeat your magical wish one more time.

OCTOBER

CELTIC MYTH

SAMHAIN

From the 31st October through to the end of the 1st November, the Celts celebrated Samhain, also known as the festival of the dead. This was a significant time for early farmers as it marked the gathering of the harvest and a return to the dark of winter. Families would extinguish their hearth fires while the crops were collected, then reunite around a communal fire lit by a spinning wheel, which represented the sun. Prayers were said and thanks were given to the gods for an abundant yield. Cattle were also sacrificed to the hungry flames to secure safe passage for the rest of the tribe through the winter months. Each member of the community was required to pay homage to their local chieftain. Refusal to make such an appearance was thought to anger the deities and lead to illness or death.

The barriers between worlds were especially thin at this time, and fires were relit from the central pyre to light the way for loved ones in spirit. It was common practice to set a place for the dearly departed at the feasting table to acknowledge their presence. While ghostly ancestors were welcomed, the fey were seen as a threat. It was feared that sneaky sprites might seize the spirits of loved ones and kidnap them. To prevent this, people would dress in their dirtiest, smelliest clothes to scare the fairies away, and keep the souls of the living safe and well.

TREE OF THE MONTH

IVY

Birth Sign Dates: 30 September - 27 October

The tenacity of the ivy was recognized by the Druids. They believed it was a powerful plant because of the way it could resist the winter frosts and thrive under the harshest conditions. Its resilience to all weathers gave it a sinister reputation, but if it grew around the entrance to a home or dwelling, it was considered a positive omen. In this case, the ivy was a symbol of protection and used to keep evil at bay. It was also thought that if ivy grew upon the grave of a woman, it was proof that she had died of a broken heart.

Those born under this tree sign always persevere, despite the odds. They know how to handle life's challenges with grace, and tend to see both sides of an argument. Ivy characters also have an inner strength and a generous soul. They are helpful and optimistic, and will always go the extra mile for a worthy cause.

CELTIC DEITY

THE MORRIGAN

Swathed in shadows and dark as night, the Morrigan stalked the battlefield waiting for the souls of the dead. This powerful goddess was revered by the Celts. A symbol of enchantment, death and rebirth, she was the goddess and guardian of the dead, and a warrior queen who stood her ground in battle. It was thought that her presence stirred the emotions and fuelled the fire of aggression, which was the cause of many wars.

A shapeshifting sorceress, the Morrigan was commonly seen in the form of a raven, picking at carcasses upon the battlefield or loitering among the rubble waiting for the dying to finally pass. She was also associated with the crow and the vulture, but had the ability to change into many different forms.

In her infamous encounter with the warrior Cú Chulainn, she transformed into a heifer, an eel and a wolf in a bid to win the fight between them. While some considered her evil, the Morrigan is a representation of the continual cycles of life and death. Her role was to guide recently passed souls on to the next life. Depictions of this goddess, often with a bird's head or feathers, appear on stone slabs and menhirs, and were also carved into armour breast plates excavated from Celtic sites throughout Europe. This is proof enough that she was a key member of the Celtic pantheon, petitioned for strength in battle and safe passage in death.

DEITY RITUAL

RITUAL TO RESTORE BALANCE

The dark side of the Morrigan is often explored in stories and myths, making her a goddess of the night and synonymous with the transition between life and death. Change of any sort is related to this deity, and she can be called upon to restore balance when you are feeling unsettled.

Harness the energy of this goddess in a simple nighttime ritual, which helps you centre yourself and calm your mind before sleep.

- ∞ Before bed, sit by a window and draw back the curtains.
- ∞ Stare out into the darkness. Don't be afraid of what you can't see. Simply breathe deeply and allow your eyes to acclimatize. Slowly and steadily, the dense blackness of night will reveal its landscape.
- ∞ As you look into the night from the safety and light of your bedroom, imagine a dark comforting cloak of feathers draped around your shoulders.
- ∞ Draw a long deep breath in and feel yourself cocooned in this warmth.
- ∞ Exhale slowly, and release any fear or tension.
- ∞ Continue to breathe in this way for at least five minutes.
- ∞ Embrace the darkness outside as it meets the lightness within your room, and say, 'Dark and light, in me meet. I am centred, at peace, complete'.

SACRED SITE

GLANUM

Saint-Rémy-de-Provence, France

This once former capital of the Glanic people can be found nestled below a gorge beneath the gaze of the Alpilles mountains. Once a fortified Celtic settlement, Glanum evolved under Roman rule into a prosperous town, although remnants of its earlier incarnation can still be seen. Originally, the Celtic tribes built a rampart and a shrine at the spring in the valley to their god Glanis. A settlement was then constructed around this central spot. The healing waters of this shrine became a focal point to which many travelled.

SYMBOL

THE WHEEL OF TARANIS

The Wheel of Taranis symbol, which is circular in structure with spokes reaching out from a central point, resembles a chariot wheel. It was associated with the Celtic god of thunder Taranis, a key member of the pantheon. The wheel formation is said to represent the cyclical nature of weather, and the god's ability to conjure a storm. A popular symbol, it featured in Celtic artwork and on coinage, and was carved into artefacts, most likely as a way of petitioning the power of the god. Being circular in shape, this symbol was also synonymous with the eternal progression of life, death and rebirth.

SYMBOL RITUAL

RITUAL FOR MOTIVATION

Use the motion of the wheel in this symbol to provide focus, motivation and swift action. The physical elements of this ritual will energize your body and mind.

You will need: a long-handled broom or mop

- ∞ Stand with your feet hip-width apart and place the broom behind your shoulders with your hands holding it in place. The broom represents the spokes of the wheel.
- ∞ Slowly begin to twist at your waist from side to side, using the broom to help you create a rhythm and momentum.
- ∞ Imagine that you're spinning like the spokes of a wheel, getting faster by the minute. Continue to rotate the broom in this way for a couple of minutes and see this physical exercise as a representation of you moving towards your goals, gaining momentum and focus as you near your target.
- ∞ When you've finished, take a minute to catch your breath, and then take the broom and begin to sweep in a circular motion around the room. You don't actually have to clean; just imagine you're clearing away stagnant energy and making space for new opportunities and movement in your life.

MONTHLY SPELL

SPELL FOR FORGIVENESS AND COMPASSION

The Celts took inspiration from the changing seasons. They followed the rhythms of nature, withdrawing to rest as the nights drew in and using the darkness to replenish the spirit and bury the past.

Look to the elements and the time of year to help you forgive, move on and find some compassion for yourself and others with this spell.

You will need: a potato, a sheet of newspaper, a potato peeler, a small trowel, a patch of earth

∞ Hold the potato in both hands and as you exhale, push any hurt, pain or anger into your outward breath. Imagine you're breathing these emotions into the potato.

∞ Practise this a couple of times and when you're ready, place the sheet of newspaper on the floor.

∞ Say, 'I peel away the pain. Let forgiveness into my heart. I shed the layers of hurt. I am ready for a new start'.

∞ Peel the skin off the potato and let the peel fall at your feet.

∞ Once the potato is peeled, put it to one side (you can save it to cook with if you like) and gather the peel.

∞ Go outside and dig a small hole using the trowel.

∞ Place the peelings in the hole, cover them with earth and say, 'I peel away the pain. Let forgiveness into my heart. I shed the layers of hurt. I am ready for a new start'.

NOVEMBER

CELTIC MYTH

THE CHILDREN OF LIR

A haunting myth with a number of variations, this tale of love, loss and dark magic is one of the most famous in the Celtic tradition.

At the dawn of time when men mixed with fairy kin, there lived a king called Lir. A member of the magical Tuatha Dé Danann, he was a kind-hearted ruler and deeply in love with his wife Aobh. Together they had four children, but tragically Aobh died while giving birth to twin boys, leaving the king bereft. In a bid to keep the family unit strong, Lir married his wife's sister Aoife. His new bride was not accustomed to having children at her feet and soon grew tired of their whining. She was jealous of the love that Lir showed them and in a fit of rage cast a spell transforming the children into four elegant swans, a curse that would last nine hundred years.

The children fled in their winged form, but whenever they passed King Lir's castle, they would sing out with such sweet, sorrowful voices that it drew their father to the riverside to be with them. While Aoife might have been satisfied with the outcome of her dark magic, her father King Bodhbh Dearg was horrified at his daughter's behaviour. He cast a spell transforming her into an air demon as penance for her deeds, and it's thought that on a stormy day when the wind howls and batters the rafters, you can still hear Aoife's mournful cries.

TREE OF THE MONTH

REED

Birth Sign Dates: 28 October - 24 November

Reeds were significant to the Druids who recognized their power, strength and flexibility. Associated with the element of wind, the Druids believed that the sound of the reeds singing as a breeze passed through them was an omen of bad weather to come. The flexibility of this broad-leafed grass with its stiff sturdy stems meant it was crucial to everyday life and used to make a variety of tools. From sacred darts and arrows to writing implements, it was also fashioned into a musical instrument similar to a flute.

Those born under this tree sign don't miss anything. They love to dig deep, whether they're getting to know someone or exploring a new hobby, and they will go out of their way to find out everything they can about their new interest. Their direct approach and love of communication and conversation makes them drawn to the fields of journalism and research.

CELTIC DEITY

DIAN CÉCHT

The son of the Dagda, Dian Cécht was one of the most respected gods of the Tuatha Dé Danann. His healing abilities meant that he took on the role of key physician, mending and fixing wounds and using his knowledge of herbs to perform a number of magical feats. Often known as the Lord of Spells, Dian Cécht had a sacred well filled with healing herbs. Imbued with the power of his chants, it could bring anyone back from the brink of death. At the end of every battle he would immerse the badly wounded into the well, letting the water consume their pain. They would bathe and emerge completely healed and ready for their next skirmish. This practice was adopted by the Celts, who believed in the power of ritual bathing.

According to Irish legend, when the god Nuadu lost his hand in the battle of Mag Tuired, Dian Cécht swiftly intervened. While he couldn't restore the entire limb, he fashioned his friend a silver hand that could move as well as a real one. Another Irish legend claims that this selfless god saved Ireland. On hearing that the Morrigan, the goddess of war and death, had a son who had three venomous snakes that had the potential to kill every mortal within his grasp, Dian leapt into action. Tackling the snakes using his magical skill, he threw them into the river. The evil poison that dripped from their fangs caused the waters to boil and they eventually drowned. This one action marked the god as a hero among the people of Ireland.

DEITY RITUAL

RITUAL TO BOOST VITALITY

Dian Cécht used the power of water combined with the healing properties of plants to restore the sick and ailing. The cleansing rituals that were inspired by this deity were used daily by the Celts, who recognized the potential of Mother Nature to soothe and heal body, mind and soul.

Follow suit and use the power of water in this bathing ritual to clear your mind and boost vitality.

You will need: a chamomile teabag, fresh sage leaves, a cup of hot water, a towel

- ∞ Run a hot bath and while the bath is running, add the chamomile teabag and a couple of fresh sage leaves into a cup and cover with hot water. The soothing properties of chamomile will ease aches and pains while calming the mind, and the addition of sage will cleanse and lift the spirits.
- ∞ Allow to brew for a few minutes.
- ∞ Remove the teabag and sage leaves and add the water to your bath water.
- ∞ Immerse yourself in the bath water and feel the warmth and the herbal scent work its magic. Relax and soak for as long as you like.
- ∞ When you're ready, emerge from the bath and give yourself a brisk towel dry. You should feel relaxed, energized and restored.

SACRED SITE

THE DROMBEG STONE CIRCLE

County Cork, Ireland

Also known as the Druid's Altar, this megalithic site is accessed by a simple track that leads to seventeen sandstone pillars arranged in a circular design. One of the stones is situated to mark the midpoint and showcases the sunrise upon the winter solstice when viewed from the hills in the distance. The rocks are arranged in order of height, with thirteen of the original pillars still standing. Excavations of the site have revealed a communal cooking pit called a *fulacht fiadh*, which dates back to around 800 BCE.

SYMBOL

SOLOMON'S KNOT

An ancient symbol with a long history of usage, Solmon's knot was a favourite of the Celts, although it was borrowed by many cultures. Like all knotwork patterns, it has no beginning or end and looks like two interlaced loops. This symbol is thought to represent the union of humankind with divinity. It's synonymous with immortality, and also seen as an emblem of faith. Some scholars believe it epitomizes true love and union of two people who, like the interlocking loops, are inseparable.

SYMBOL RITUAL

RITUAL TO STRENGTHEN A BOND

Use a simplified version of this knot in this visualization to cement the bonds of love and friendship in any type of relationship. The interlaced loops of this symbol promote unity when used alongside a positive affirmation.

- ∞ Find a comfortable spot to sit and spend a few minutes breathing deeply to calm and clear your mind.
- ∞ Close your eyes and picture two giant loops interlaced upon the floor. See the image shining in your mind.
- ∞ Imagine standing in one of the loops. As you look across at the other loop, imagine you see the person you want to connect with. Together you are connected, standing within this symbol.
- ∞ Breathe deeply and say, 'The bonds between us are strong and true. Love is flowing between me and you'.
- ∞ When you're ready, let the image fade and slowly open your eyes.

MONTHLY SPELL

SPELL TO PROTECT YOU WHEN YOU'RE FEELING VULNERABLE

The Celts used standing stones to raise energy for worship and to celebrate each solstice and equinox. The stones were positioned in a circular design to reflect the continuous cycles of life, and to create a sacred and powerful space. Harness the power of the elements and the circular shape of the standing stones with this spell, which will help you feel protected.

You will need: five white candles of the same height and shape, an item of jewellery that you wear often, a lighter or matches

- ∞ Arrange the white candles in a large circle to represent a stone circle. The candles represent purity and light.
- ∞ Place the item of jewellery in the centre of the circle. This will represent you.
- ∞ Light each candle and look at the circle of light that you have created.
- ∞ Take three slow deep breaths. On the third breath as you exhale, say, 'I create a dome of light and love, a place where I am safe from harm. Protected, shielded from bad vibes, I am safe, strong, relaxed and calm'.
- ∞ Spend a few minutes watching the candles burn and then repeat the magical chant in your mind or out loud.
- ∞ To finish, extinguish the candles and retrieve your jewellery. Wear it whenever you need to feel safe and protected.

THE CELTIC YEAR AT A GLANCE

WINTER	DECEMBER	JANUARY	FEBRUARY
FOLKLORE/MYTH/ FESTIVAL	FOLKLORE: ALBAN ARTHAN	MYTH: THE ANKOU	FESTIVAL: IMBOLC
TREE	ELDER	BIRCH AND ROWAN	ASH
CELTIC DEITY	CERIDEWEN	DANU	THE CAILLEACH
DEITY RITUAL	RITUAL FOR PSYCHIC POWERS	RITUAL FOR SELF CARE AND ENERGY	RITUAL FOR POSITIVITY
SACRED SITE	FANUM D'ARON	THE CARNAC STANDING STONES	ST BRIGID'S WELL
SYMBOL	CELTIC CROSS	THE AWEN	ST BRIGID'S CROSS
SYMBOL RITUAL	RITUAL FOR STRENGTH AND PURPOSE	RITUAL FOR CREATIVITY	RITUAL FOR REJUVINATION
MONTHLY SPELL	SPELL TO PROMOTE HARMONY AND GOOD FORTUNE	SPELL FOR INNER STRENGTH AND PROTECTION	SPELL FOR GOOD FORTUNE AND TO ATTRACT BLESSINGS

SPRING	MARCH	APRIL	MAY
FOLKLORE/TRADITION/ FESTIVAL	FOLKLORE: TREE NYMPHS	TRADITION: BARDS, OVATES AND DRUIDS	FESTIVAL: BALTANE
TREE	ALDER	WILLOW	HAWTHORN
CELTIC DEITY	RHIANNON	LUGH	ÁINE
DEITY RITUAL	RITUAL TO RELEASE THE PAST	RITUAL FOR ABUNDANCE	RITUAL FOR SELF-LOVE
SACRED SITE	THE PRINCE OF GLAUBERG STATUE	GRIANÁN OF AILEACH	THE SOURCE OF THE SEINE
SYMBOL	DARA KNOT	THE TREE OF LIFE	TRISKELION
SYMBOL RITUAL	RITUAL FOR RESILIENCE	RITUAL TO RECHARGE AND BOOST ENERGY	RITUAL TO DEAL WITH STRESS
MONTHLY SPELL	SPELL TO CALM THE MIND AND BOOST PERSONAL POWER	SPELL TO PROMOTE JOY AND ATTRACT POSITIVE ENERGY	SPELL TO PROMOTE NEW GROWTH IN ANY AREA OF LIFE

SUMMER	JUNE	JULY	AUGUST
TRADITION	DIVINATION TECHNIQUES	THE OTHER-WORLD	LUGHNASADH
TREE	OAK	HOLLY	HAZEL
CELTIC DEITY	THE DAGDA	CERNUNNOS	SULIS
DEITY RITUAL	RITUAL TO ATTRACT PROSPERITY	RITUAL TO GENERATE NEW WEALTH	RITUAL FOR SELF-HEALING
SACRED SITE	BRÚ NA BÓINNE	THE DANUBE RIVER	MADRON WELL
SYMBOL	THE AILM	THE SINGLE SPIRAL	THE MOTHERHOOD KNOT
SYMBOL RITUAL	RITUAL FOR CALM	RITUAL FOR DISCOVERY	RITUAL FOR GRATITUDE
MONTHLY SPELL	SPELL TO CENTRE YOURSELF AND CREATE BALANCE	SPELL TO CONNECT WITH YOUR ANIMALS	SPELL FOR PEACE AND HEALING

AUTUMN	SEPTEMBER	OCTOBER	NOVEMBER
MYTH	THE SALMON OF KNOWLEDGE	SAMHAIN	THE CHILDREN OF LIR
TREE	THE VINE	IVY	REED
CELTIC DEITY	AENGUS ÓG	THE MORRIGAN	DIAN CÉCHT
DEITY RITUAL	RITUAL FOR NEW LOVE	RITUAL TO RESTORE BALANCE	RITUAL TO BOOST VITALITY
SACRED SITE	GAER FAWR	GLANUM	THE DROMBEG STONE CIRCLE
SYMBOL	THE TRIQUETRA	THE WHEEL OF TARANIS	SOLOMON'S KNOT
SYMBOL RITUAL	RITUAL FOR PERSONAL POWER	RITUAL FOR MOTIVATION	RITUAL TO STRENGTHEN A BOND
MONTHLY SPELL	SPELL TO BOOST INSIGHT AND INCREASE INTUITION	SPELL FOR FORGIVENESS AND COMPASSION	SPELL TO PROTECT YOU WHEN YOU'RE FEELING VULNERABLE

ABOUT THE AUTHOR

A professional storyteller with a keen interest in mythology, spirituality and the natural world, Alison Davies is the author of over sixty books, including *The Mystical Year, The Lunar Year* and *The Self-Care Year*. She also runs writing workshops at universities across the United Kingdom.

ACKNOWLEDGEMENTS

I would like to thank the wonderful team at Quadrille for helping to create such a special book. In particular, I'd like thank my editors Sofie Shearman and Oreolu Grillo for their talent and skill, the designer Katy Everett for helping to shape my words and make them stand out on the page, and also the wonderful illustrator, Megan Ivy Griffiths, for the magical illustrations.

Quadrille, Penguin Random House UK, One Embassy Gardens,
8 Viaduct Gardens, London SW11 7BW

Quadrille Publishing Limited is part of the Penguin Random House group of companies whose addresses can be found at global.penguinrandomhouse.com

Penguin
Random House
UK

Published by Quadrille in 2025

www.penguin.co.uk

A CIP catalogue record for this book is available from the British Library

ISBN 978 1 83783 2866

10 9 8 7 6 5 4 3 2 1

MANAGING DIRECTOR
Sarah Lavelle

EDITORIAL DIRECTOR
Kate Pollard

ASSISTANT EDITOR
Sofie Shearman

ASSISTANT EDITOR
Oreolu Grillo

DESIGNER
Katy Everett

ILLUSTRATOR
Megan Ivy Griffiths

HEAD OF PRODUCTION
Stephen Lang

PRODUCTION MANAGER
Sabeena Atchia

Colour reproduction by p2d

Printed in China by C&C Offset Printing Co., Ltd.

The authorized representative in the EEA is Penguin Random House Ireland, Morrison Chambers, 32 Nassau Street, Dublin D02 YH68.

FSC www.fsc.org MIX Paper | Supporting responsible forestry FSC® C018179

Penguin Random House is committed to a sustainable future for our business, our readers and our planet. This book is made from Forest Stewardship Council® certified paper.